The Altar of Innocence

Also by New Academia Publishing

THE MAN WHO GOT AWAY: Poems, by Grace Cavalieri

IN BLACK BEAR COUNTRY, by Maureen Waters

ALWAYS THE TRAINS: Poems, by Judy Neri

Read an excerpt at **www.newacademia.com**

2021

To Lois + Mike —
Thanks for all
of your support over
the years.

The Altar of Innocence

Fondly,
Ann

Poems by Ann Bracken

NEW ACADEMIA PUBLISHING   SCARITH

Washington, DC

Library of Congress Control Number: 2014958768
ISBN 978-0-9906939-5-6 paperback (alk. paper)

SCARI/H An imprint of New Academia Publishing

New Academia Publishing
PO Box 27420, Washington, DC 20038-7420
info@newacademia.com - www.newacademia.com

Cover image: Watercolor fashion design, "Sheer Elegance," by Dorothy Wetzler, 1935

For my children, Brian and Christella

"...and there was a new voice
which you slowly
recognized as your own,
that kept you company
as you strode deeper and deeper
into the world,
determined to do
the only thing you could do--
determined to save
the only life you could save."

~Mary Oliver, "The Journey"

Contents

Preface   x
Acknowledgements   xi

I   1
Helen's Choices, 1937   3
Helen Lives The Queen-For-a-Day Life   4
Postpartum   5
Prayers to Mary, Queen of Heaven   6
Notes On the Kitchen Table   7
Unraveling   9
The Altar of Innocence   10
The Pediatrician   11

II   13
Mirror, Mirror   15
Nested   17
Martini Memories   18
Wine and Water   19
Love Is   20
Summer Storm   21
Mrs. S   23
Adultery   24
The Swimming Pool Ladies   26
Three Days, Three Nights   27

When Medals Are Useless   29
The Same   31
If It's Saturday, There's Meatloaf for Dinner   33
Time Travel   34
Why Is It Called a Miraculous Medal?   35
Intervention   36
Perspective   37
Confession at Sixteen   38
Design   39
When I Think Of My Father   40
Postcards   41
I Can Finally Hear My Mother   42

III   43
Notes on the Table   45
Almost Athens   47
Stubborn Guests   48
Diagnosis   50
Bike Ride   51
Kite Without A String   52
My Husband Tells Me How He Feels   53
The Long Trajectory of Therapy Starts with Questions   55
Afternoon Resolve   56
The Cobalt Valley   58
Advice   59
Day Treatment   60
The Shock Machine   62
This Is An Outpatient Facility   63
The Hopkins Doctor Diagnoses Me   65
My Friends Insist That I'm Overmedicated   67
Even Now   69

The Energy Healer   71
When Rivers Decide   73
What Lies Beneath   74
The Final Demand   75
The Portal   76
Repurposed   77

About the Author   79

Preface

The Altar of Innocence is a book about claiming your voice. The poems in this volume, based on events in my life, explore the 60s' culture of secrecy surrounding alcoholism and depression and their effects on the young girl who witnessed the roller-coaster ride of mental illness and self-medication. In writing these poems, I spent time analyzing my parents' unspoken lessons—about communication, conflict, and managing illness—and how those lessons unfolded in my own marriage. I explore these issues through three lenses: conjectures about what my mother might have felt, recollections of key events in my childhood and adolescence, and my own journey to overcome depression, heal from chronic migraines, and finally leave a destructive marriage.

By mining the daily journal I kept during the four years of my depression, I was able to select key events to illustrate my story, as well as the records of medications, conversations, and feelings that I had during that time.

I offer my story as a glimpse into the secret worlds that so many still inhabit today. We are never as alone as we think.

Ann Bracken
October, 2014

Acknowledgments

Gunpowder Review: "Postcards"

Life in Me Like Grass on Fire: Love Poems: "The Pediatrician"

Little Patuxent Review: "Wine and Water", "Adultery"

Praxilla: "Martini Memories", "Stubborn Guests"

Reckless Writing: The Modernization of Poetry by Emerging Writers of the 21st Century: "Mrs. S"

Scribble: "Nested", "The Portal"

I would like to thank the following people for their steadfast belief in my work and for their professional guidance with my manuscript: Grace Cavalieri, Laura Shovan, Patricia VanAmburg, Danuta Hinc, Jane Elkins, Kimberly Becker, and Kristine Daniel.

I

Helen's Choice, 1937

Did my mother ever weigh her options?
Sometimes I look at her designs,
try to tease out the answer
to a puzzle I can never solve.

Was it the way my father's hand
secured
the small of her back
that signaled he was the one for her?

Was it his plans for their life together—
safety, security— that Mark promised
as he slipped a square-cut diamond
on to her slender finger?

I can almost hear my grandmother mutter
Helen, don't put your faith in dreams
as she spies my grandfather tuck a pencil behind his ear
and head to the track again.

Did Mom's design instructor encourage her to pursue her gifts?
Helen, dream of dancing in that dress
Pointing to the canvas, prodding, suggesting—
imagine how silk flows, how velvet shimmers.

When potential collided with practical,
my mother chose Mark's hand.
When she tucked her designer dreams into brown cardboard—
was she hoping for a later rendezvous
with her other love?

Helen Lives The Queen-For-a-Day Life

There is no pattern for the life she's living—She cannot render sense
out of the daily chores—diapers and meals,
homework and toddlers. There is no pasture
behind her house like the golden field in the Wyeth painting.

Her dreams play in the shadows like rogue relatives
who squander security for passion. Sometimes she feels
degrees away from sanity, like when she imagines her dusty art portfolios
whimpering in the basement buried—

perhaps under the twigs of youthful dreams.
She plays at being happy as she peels another diaper off her infant son,
cajoles vegetables into her daughters' stubborn mouths.
She feels her spirit wither even as her husband cheers her

news of another pregnancy and measures out an ounce of gin
for her nightly martini.

Postpartum

While the three older children
sleep upstairs,
Helen sits in the wooden-slatted rocker
nursing her youngest,
blond and plump,
snuggled to her chest.

She hears her mother's voice thunder,
What more do you want, Helen?
as she rocks, stifled and empty,
in the dawn-colored room.

As her daughter dozes,
she places her silently in the
barred white crib,
then finds herself collapsed

solitary in her bed—
cold now,
after her husband has gone to work.
Wanting the sweet relief
of wine in her veins,

and a permanent heavy slumber
to fill the void,
she pulls the covers over her head
crying mutely for rescue.

Prayers to Mary, Queen of Heaven

The children finish grace,
gobble their warm grilled cheese sandwiches
before she can pour the milk—
Their little tummies round
under faded swimsuits.

A spasm of guilt shivers
through her body as she waves good-bye
shielded behind the screen.
She watches them skip down the street holding hands
placing penny-bets on who will do the first flip.

Hail Mary, where is the grace
I beg for, just to get through each hour?
She feels the neighbors' eyes bore into her, imagining
their innuendos cresting into a chorus of "Bad mother, bad
mother"
until she slams the door on the third day this week
her children walk to the pool alone.

Holy Mother, why do I drag my limp body into bed just after noon?
She closes her eyes, imagining her children
splashing in the water, diving into the pool.
Dear Jesus, Son of God, help me to get up before they come home.
Give me an answer when they beg,
"Please, Mom, swim with us. Just once."

Notes On the Kitchen Table

May, 1965
I have just
taken 50 sleeping
pills—can't
stand it any
longer—Somebody
must do some-
thing for me
~Helen

May, 1966
Dear Ann,
I hate to
leave you with
everything. You
are such a wonderful
daughter & I love
you so much!
I don't know
when I'll be
home if Dad
wants to lock
up that's okay.
~Mom

January, 1968
Mark, I am angry,
frustrated &
disappointed besides
being very anxious

about coming
nightwork. You
are not here
so I can't tell
you how I feel
but am going
to sleep with
the hope I'll
wake up feeling better.
~Helen

Unraveling

Thuds in the night
bumps on the head
afternoon beers
measured cocktails.

Extra booze tucked in
to pill bottles
stashed in purses
and suitcases.

Watered down wine
Mom's sluggish walk
middle of the night
whispered concerns.

Dad's furtive calls to her psychiatrist
My wife's given up, then
She's getting better, Please,
one more prescription.

Friends walk away.
Dad's off to work.
Kids sit in school.
Life is outside

sunshine and trees —
living room
clouds
hovering dark.

The Altar of Innocence

Dad is on the phone again
talking to someone
about pressing decisions, uncertain returns.

Grandma, full-busted and corseted,
bustles in the front door
tacitly assumes command of the household.

She lifts the whimpering infant from the bassinette
and wraps her in solid, fleshy arms.
Rocking side to side, she quiets the baby's cries, soothes her hunger
with a bottle of warm formula. Urgently

Dad ushers Grandma into the kitchen
and closes the door.
Huddled and silent, the trio of kids
hears the familiar bolt of the lock.

Straining at the door for a clue,
they catch vague promises
that their mother will be all right.

The children keep a silent vigil
and place their unasked questions
on the altar of their innocence.

The Pediatrician

I tell the doctor how my stomach
aches each morning,
all through school.
More breakfast, the doctor says,
turns to my father.

But deep in my
seven year old's body,
I know that more cereal and toast
can't take the place of my mother's
Chanel Number 5 clinging—
to her, to me—like a silk scarf.

More breakfast will never replace her arm
snuggled around my waist
as we read *Caps for Sale*
side by side on the sofa.

As he walks out the door,
the doctor asks my father
How's your wife and the new baby girl?
Looking back over their shoulders

and smiling sadly at me,
they tell stories
about someone who is nervous
and someone breaking down.

II

Mirror, Mirror

Mirror, mirror everywhere
she steps through the looking glass
with a compact tucked into
the patch-pockets of her girlish dreams.

In a world of Snow White queens
and Cinderella gowns
mirrors lined every wall—words
conjured magical friends, taunting

Just look at yourself!
Stop looking at yourself.
What are you looking at now?
Who are you looking for?

Barely six, she was reading fairy tales
and memorizing commandments—
while teachers warned of sin and sacrifice.

One morning, she sat
brushing her hair 100 strokes—
the ticket to Breck-perfect looks.

Peering into the mirror,
she spied her much-older and wiser brother
approaching with a smile.

Bending down, resting his chin
on her shoulder, catching her gaze, he said
"Vain, vain, vain—such a vain little girl."

She knew a curse
when she heard one.
Fingering the silver compact tucked into

her pocket, the magical gift
shape-shifted into a cruel burden.

Nested

Grandma at 98 sits rocking on the porch,
a proud Russian doll of wisdom.
Soft cataracts veil the decaying street
where she and her husband
courted under the buttery moon.

Inside the old one, the unflinching widow
who steers the family business,
fear and pain corseted under dark rayon dress.
Her tears water cottage roses
thorny sentinels of loss.

Inside the widow, the young wife
her tired rosary tucked into apron pocket—
she rocks flu-fevered babies
in an all-night vigil
behind quarantine's crimson doors.

Inside the young wife, the schoolgirl with auburn braids,
dark eyes searching for sunlight.
High above Baltimore in flames, she stands sentry on John Street,
nods in somber gratitude to the smoke-weary firemen
who stare into the haze.

When I'm afraid, I see Grandma at 70
fearless in the ocean, white swim cap protecting fuzzy gray hair.
She stands sideways
blunting the tide
inviting me in.

Martini Memories

I never understood the allure of those martinis
served with tiny green olives or slippery pearl onions.

I remember the ritual of the pour,
the tall-stemmed glasses held out by eager hands
the toasting to another family holiday on Atlanta Avenue.

I remember how the pitch of conversation
shifted from polite hellos to the debates over civil rights
and that awful Democrat in the White House.

I remember how my uncle would grab my arm as I walked by—
his wet kiss planted too long on my cheek.
I remember the smell of his martini mouth.

I remember my soft-spoken mother
finding a new voice at about one-and-a-half martinis
nibbling on naked carrot sticks, counting calories
while she nursed her drink and eyed Dad
every time she topped off her martini.

I remember how the mood shifted from jokes to jibes
unleashing veiled anger and rage.
But always the martini in hand
buffering the stinging arrows of jealousy and resentment.

The holidays at Grandma's were predictable —
always sliced carrots
always sour cream and onion dip.
And always the martinis.

Wine and Water

I am in the basement laundry room
piled high with crates
of discarded skates, broken toys,
pieces of wood to fix the just-in-case.

As I round the corner,
I glance to my left and see Dad
pouring water into a clear plastic funnel
jammed yet teetering

in a gallon-sized jug
of my mother's white wine.
He catches a glimpse of me—
turns back to the mixing and commands,

Don't ever tell your mother what you saw.
I feel as if some invisible barrier is in place
with me and Dad on one side of knowing
and my mom on the other.

Nodding in obedience, I agree, then run outside to play
swinging back and forth
between truth and loyalty
swinging higher
afraid to jump.

Love Is

I imagine myself a brunette Haley Mills singing
You've got high-igh hopes, high-igh hopes, big dapple die in the sky-ey
hopes
I curtsy,
anticipate my family's applause.

That's great, Ann, too bad you can't manage to get the words right.
Dad sips his coffee, siblings pounce on the flaw,
bored children poking fingers
into a small hole
and wiggling them around
until the tear
turns to a jagged rip.

My open smile turns to a closed grin.
A single tear slides down my cheek.
Dad slams his cup on the china saucer, shakes his head.
You're too sensitive.
Stop crying or I'll give you something to cry about.

I tuck my chin tight into my chest to still the quiver,
lower my eyes, squeeze them hard to stop the tears.
After forever, Dad and my siblings laugh and hug me. They slap
me on the back—
You know we love you. It's all just a joke.

Summer Storm

The basement was cool that July morning—
my sister hummed as she laid her doll
in the blue wooden bed,
covered her with a tiny quilt.

I brushed my doll's hair, opened the miniature dresser drawer
to pick out her outfit for the day.
Later we would sit our dolls at the wooden table
and feed them bacon and eggs for breakfast.

Outside, a push-mower whirred as our neighbor cut the grass.
Birds sang their morning song. The air cool and damp.

Like a summer storm, my mother thundered
down the wooden stairs in her saddle shoes.
I can't stand this mess anymore.
Then she stooped down and shoved the dressers into a corner.

"Mom, please, we'll make our playroom neat."
The storm gathered speed.
Mom scooped up the doll beds and dumped them into a card-
board box.
"Mom, please, just let us keep the dolls."

Spinning around, she scanned the room
then ripped the doll out of my sister's hands.
My sister hugged her knees and put her head down.
Then Mom turned to me.

Her fingers tugged at mine as if prying open a stuck latch.
You're too old to play with dolls.
"But Mom, I just turned eight."
I can't stand the mess.

The storm subsided.
Mom hauled the box full of dolls,
dressers, and beds up the stairs
and slammed the basement door.

With all the mess behind her,
she dumped the box on the curb
for the trash men
and headed out to weed her flower beds.

Mrs. S

No one ever tells the story
of Mrs. Sisyphus
perhaps because she
endures at the bottom
of the hill
with all the little boulders
 tumbling from above.
In between the spinning of cloth
and the baking of bread,
she rolls the children out the door
to play and rolls the food
home from the market.
Day after day
she jostles the water jugs
from well to house
and back .

She nudges and cajoles the
bigger boulders of animals
from pasture to barn
and finally to slaughter.
Preparing feasts
for all the Baby Sisiphi
who gather around the table
whining, *When is Daddy coming home?*

Adultery

A room full of seven year-olds
are memorizing the ten commandments.
They sit, eyes fixed on illustrated
poster-sized pages, bound
with *thou shalts* and
thou shalt nots printed
in bold block letters.

Sister speaks, the class repeats,
The sixth commandment is
Thou shalt not commit adultery.
The class echoes back, as she rushes on,
but in the space between
I raise my hand and ask,

"Sister, what's adultery?"
Furiously flipping the page, she intones,
"The *seventh* commandment is..."
My cheeks burning,
I study each word
Thou shalt not commit adultery.

I struggle toward a solid conclusion:
If adult means you are a grown-up,
adultery must mean you're
pretending to be a grown-up.
A commandment just for children.

With the realization of
my frequent sinning, I begin

examining my conscience:
How often have I played dress-up?
or pretended to be a doctor,
a nurse, a teacher?

Mental tally held in my memory, I join
my classmates filing into the church
lit solely by the red flame
of the sanctuary candle
burning for our sins.

Forty second graders cram into four pews
silently waiting to seek
forgiveness in the
velvet-curtained confessional.
The murmurs of transgressions
like incense fill the air.

I kneel, make the sign of the cross,
then stammer, "Bless me, Father,
for I have sinned. This is my first confession
and I have lied to my parents about 20 times,
fought with my brothers and sisters about 17 times,
and committed adultery 35 times."

After a brief silence punctuated by a sigh,
Father Riley assigns my penance—
two Hail Marys and one Our Father.
Leaving me to believe in
the truth of my innocence,
he forgives me all my sins.

The Swimming Pool Ladies

Mom's friend Janice with the skinny legs,
thinning hair and raspy voice
is always at the pool with the other swimming pool ladies.

Mom's friends sit together, tanned and hatted—
laughing at grown-up jokes—
lined up paper-doll perfect on the wooden loungers.

I pass by them on my way to the deep end
and stare at the empty chaise lounge where my mother should be.
The swimming pools ladies shake their heads and gossip

I hear Helen's in the hospital again...those poor children.
Stepping to the edge of the deep end,
I notice Janice lock eyes with me as I dive into the pool.

Escaping into the kick, stroke, breathe of the crawl,
moving away from her stare,
I long for my mother's smile to catch me at the other end.

Three Days, Three Nights

"...after your parents float
through the tangible
horizon and their spirits
have become part of you"
~Diane Frank

I struggle to understand my father
who sometimes returns home from work dark and silent.

My home, my life, so unlike the books I read in school
where the laughing children run to greet the suited and hatted
father
who smiles and plays with them in the yard.

My dad comes home and ignores everyone but his wife,
kissing her briefly on the lips, hugging her as if passing in a
dance.
Then he locks himself in the kitchen
and pours whiskey and soda into a highball glass.

Later our family gathers around the table in silence
punctuated by a rote blessing and the noiseless sharing of food.
All attempts at conversation with Dad yield a brief nod and a
sharp
Get your elbows off the table. Why is the kitchen floor so sticky?

After scraping the pudding cups
for the only sweetness dinner would hold,
we children know to tiptoe away from the table
and sit alone at our desks doing homework.

At bedtime, I creep back downstairs and find Dad alone in the living room
barricaded behind his newspaper and Mom, comforted by her rosary,
alone in their bedroom, hanging her head, wringing her hands.
My good-night hugs are not returned by either parent.

In time I discover that Dad's silent storms linger
for three days and three nights
until the invisible boulder in front of his heart
mysteriously rolls away at sunrise.

When Medals Are Useless

You sit alone in the hospital waiting room and
watch the second hand tick-tick-tick away the hours.
You want someone to peek into the rectangle window of the
swinging door and say
Such a brave girl. You're not even crying.

You wrap your white corduroy jacket tight as a tourniquet
hoping for relief
but the thud of something heavy falling in the corridor
opens the flood of images again.

Your father yells
Wake up and get in here.
You shoot out of bed and stand in the doorway
of the bathroom, see your mother hanging over the sink—

thin yellow towels bind her wrists.
Bent over and silent, she doesn't see you
as she stares at her blood rivering down the drain
and staining her nylon nightgown with red blooms.

You move closer to rub her back.
Mom's got her Miraculous Medal pinned over her left breast
but it seems useless now.

Dad pushes past both of you to the phone
tells someone you'll be there soon but he gives a fake name.
Nothing is making sense. Then

you find yourself in your parents' bedroom
pulling a dress over your mother's soaked nightgown
and stuffing her limp feet into loafers.

Dad props Mom in the front seat of the car
you sit alone in the back seat of the blue Plymouth
and close your eyes to the streetlights.

The Same

Part One

The day after your younger brother and sister cleaned up the mess
in the bathroom—
that's what everyone calls the blood on the floor, the red-stained
towels and rugs,
the splotches on the tile, the crimson trails left in the tub.
The day after you spend half the night in the hospital
with your mother who slit her wrists
and your father who folds all of his words
the way he folds his dollar bills and sticks them neatly into his
wallet—
Everything is the same.
The same florescent-lit kitchen, the same bowls of cereal,
the same dad frying bacon and eggs for breakfast,
the same empty space at the table
where your mother will sit after the family is gone.

You wear the same school uniform, ride the same city bus,
filled with the same people who get on at the same stop every day.
You climb the same slate steps,
pull open the same wrought-iron barred doors
smile at the same friends.

You act the same all day, maybe a little more quiet than usual,
but you are a serious girl, so no one really notices.
You ride the same bus home, get off at the same stop.
Enter the house through the same back door.
See the empty kitchen table, check on your mother who naps in
her bedroom.
The same except for the white gauze bandages on her wrists.

Part Two

You race down the black iron steps,
tear through the field behind your house,
pound on your best-friend's front door.
Saying nothing, you run upstairs and tell her you need to talk
and it's private so you close the door.

Now you are safe.
Now you can cry the tears dammed inside for nearly 24 hours.
Now you can feel.
She hugs you as you weep into her blouse.
She doesn't know what to do with your pain, so both of you
tuck the secret away in the same rote fashion
as you tuck in your uniform blouse every morning.

Part Three

Calmer now, you walk home through the same field
and climb the same black iron steps.
You fix a simple dinner, then your father walks in the front door,
hangs up his hat on the same hook
fixes the same highball he drinks every day after work.
He checks on your sleeping mother,
then sits in the same chair where he always reads his paper.

When you call the family to dinner
your mother's place at the table is empty.
All of you murmur the same grace and then silently eat your meal.
Everything is the same until your father puts his head in his hands
and sobs.

If It's Saturday, There's Meatloaf for Dinner

If it's Wednesday, I need to clean.
Mom never skips a chore—each week
she straps on her thick rubber knee-pads
scrubs the floors with Spic and Span.

If it's 2 o'clock, I need to take a nap.
After Mom places the black telephone on a cushion,
she grabs a beer and retreats to her darkened bedroom.
At the stroke of 5 o'clock, wine with Dad. Wine again at 11 to summon
sleep.

If it's Saturday, there's meatloaf for dinner.
Mom uses her hands and squishes the chopped onions,
egg, celery seed, tomato soup, and ground beef into a loaf. She follows
recipes to the last quarter teaspoon.

Over and over Mom falls down the stairs in the middle of the night.
Sometimes stitches for the gashes in her forehead, sometimes a bandaid.
Most nights, Dad sits in his chair, shielded behind the *Daily Pilot.*
"All I want is peace and quiet."

Time Travel

I want to go back
to my mother who wrote
those desperate notes and left them
on the kitchen table.

Back to the woman
who tried to quench
her sacred thirst
with ordinary
Gallo wine.

I want to push
all of her pill bottles
off the counter and cheer as they crash.
Then I will show her
the dresses she designed—
those watercolors
from her lost self.

Maybe I could even
lead her up to the roof
where we would sit together
touching the green of trees
and Mom could see that anything is possible.

Why Is It Called a Miraculous Medal?

Nothing miraculous ever happens even after
four years of slipping on Mary's medal every morning—
a mandatory part of my uniform.

So far, Mary, you haven't saved me from nuns
who disparage my questions as bold and brazen.
Who condemn my unbuttoned collar, my rolled skirt.

No, and you haven't protected me from the taunts of the cool girls
who descend like Harpies on all of us quiet ones
peck away at us when we miss their jokes. They feast on our naiveté.

Even my mother, with her Miraculous Medal pinned to her nylon
nightgown.
Mom of the bowed head, the gasping breaths,
the wringing hands—

How about a miracle for her?

Intervention

It's going to be simple
clean and neat, like in the high school psych textbook.

I'll talk to Mom about her alcoholism
tell her it's not her fault, she has a disease.

All she has to do is go to AA meetings
and stop drinking.

But I don't know about the
bomb shelter of her illness

where Mom hides from
her fear and loneliness.

I don't know about
the clusters of rationalization

stored in the darkness
like the endless brown sacks of potatoes

served up as a routine part of dinner
night after night.

*Mom, we'll go to meetings together
and you'll be just fine.*

I didn't know about her
mantle of shame.

When it's time to take her to the meeting,
Mom tells me
Daddy says I'm not an alcoholic.

Perspective

In the glimpse back over my shoulder
my mother matches paint chips to drapery fabric,
a Renoir hangs over the sofa.
In the half-turn of reflection,
Mom ties the sash of my party dress with a perfect bow.

If I could push open the door
to my childhood home, call out to my mother
I'd find her sitting
in the yellow kitchen
shelling peas into a colander.

Or if it's Saturday
Mom is rolling out the pie dough into a perfect circle.
I sit next to her as she folds under the edges of the crust
then finger-pinches the chilled dough into a thick border.
In the half-turn of her face
I see an artist at play.

Confession At Sixteen

His bedroom smells of Brut aftershave and pressed shirts.
The Rolling Stones thump thump thump in the background
He pulls me next to him on the bed.

I like kissing him
even though he teases
You're a little chubby, but you're cute.

 I feel his tongue force its way into my mouth,
he sighs as he tugs my blouse out of the waistband and
inches his fingers under the white cotton fabric.

He pauses at my waist and when I don't
push him away, he keeps going.
I don't want him to touch my breasts

but it still feels good and
then my whole body tingles
when he squeezes them
and traces my lips with his tongue.

 I leave his house
 and drive straight to confession.
 Bless me father, for I have sinned.
 I don't know how to say no.

Design

Dad's veined hands dig through boxes
in the basement storage room.
A faded art portfolio fills the space between boxes
and spills its magic like wisps of sheer fabric.
Just some stuff of your mother's.
Dad brushes aside her watercolor designs—
The real treasure is your grandfather's poems.

"And Mom's designs?
Sure, sure, they're all yours.

I select five designs—take them to a framing shop.
The owner and I sort through dozens of possibilities
until my hands are drawn to mats covered in muted fabrics and
frames that echo the arcs and angles of Mom's 30s fashions.

Weeks later, I commandeer the living room
clear some shelves, arrange the framed dress designs—a makeshift
gallery.
My mother, always patient, smiles when she sees me
asks no questions when I brush her hair, change her blouse, apply
fresh lipstick.
Her eyes closed in anticipation, I wheel her in to the exhibit.
Mom smiles, squeezes my hand.

Her designs framed in silver Art Deco
matted in pale linen.

When I Think Of My Father

It's as if my legs are pumping up and down
riding faster
back to

all the mornings
when Dad cooked
breakfast for us in the yellow kitchen.

I hear eggs sizzling in the cast iron skillet
smell Eskay bacon and Taylor's ham,
hear Dad ask, *Can I make you anything?*

When I think of my father, the rub of regret
wraps its hands around me
as if to strangle my answer

and offer a new scene
where I slide the yogurt container
back into the refrigerator

and instead
I say yes to the eggs fried in bacon grease,
dotted with the bite of black pepper.

Postcards

Dad held a stack of postcards,
old and faded
hand-painted and sepia-toned
of Mt. Rushmore, The Great Salt Lake,
and The Smokey Mountains.

He pressed them into my palm,
along with his fatherly trust.
Ann, they're stamped and addressed.
Just drop a line to your mother
and me. Have a good time.

I was all of twenty—
another curly-haired hippie chick—
leaving on a cross-country Odyssey
in a blue Chevy van.

I loved Dad, but inside I was laughing.
Yet Dad's postcards became part of a
weekly routine, a lifeline of connection,
forged in the ritual of writing postcards
by the light of a Coleman lantern.

Years later, after Dad is gone,
I feel the tether of trust
connecting me with my father across time's borders.
I find a hand-tinted card featuring Mt. Rushmore,
but postmarked St. Louis, scribbled with my notes
about the swaying Arch across the Mississippi.

I Can Finally Hear My Mother

The great grief cry that rises
out of your buried portfolios
The screams of *Just let me be.*
The rage when no one
would listen—until finally
meal after meal ended with choking
and gagging. You coughed until red-faced, gasping for air.
And I can still feel the old ladies in the nursing home
grabbing my arm as I walked towards you. I still hear them pleading,
We're so worried about your mother. This coughing after every meal.

And when the soft walls of your throat narrowed
and fused with cancer, it was too late
to hear your voice.

How long had the cancer been growing
moving into your lungs, filling your stomach.
Now that you are gone I can see all the times
you tried to tell us—
choking back the pain
straining for breath to say
the words I can only imagine.

III

Notes on the Table

Mom set the breakfast table
placed her silent paper offerings
on Dad's plate.

Dear Mark,
Last night was
the first time I've
tried to put a little
whiskey on top of
a little wine since
way last time.
I am very strict
about taking only 1 ½ oz.
& 1 capful at 5:30
on the dot.
From now on I'll
take beer at night.
Is that okay? Helen

Dad's answer—a note on her plate.

As children, we watched the back and forth of their tattered
correspondence.
We learned that spoken words could shatter the calm of our home's
icy crust.
When we squabbled, Dad warned, *Stop fighting*
You want to send your mother back to the hospital?

Now my husband and I wrap our battles and negotiation in paper.
Words anchored like tentative footholds
across blue glaciers of silence.
My hands slippery with fear.

Another home made and unmade
by words on the page.

Almost Athens

Annapolis evening, blue harbor, empty masts
like white skippers with folded wings.

Nineteen summers, I imagine myself in Athens. June equinox
moon suspended, a lone pearl between my breasts

In the back seat of his mother's Plymouth
he places a pillow under my head.

I wait for trumpets announcing surrender.
Equal passion, equal pain.

When it's over, bodies twined
like silver chains, he grabs my

belly flesh, tells me to lose those doughy rolls
if I ever want another trip to Athens.

Stubborn Guests

I. "You'll Never"

       rocks your bed in the middle of the night,
slips her icy hands over your eyes,
jerks the comforter to the floor,
and stamps around the room
with her invisible muddy boots

II. "You Can't"

       cruises in around 5am
just as the *Washington Post*
slams into the top step
of your cement stoop.
She parks herself
outside your door
and flicks stones at you
when you reach for the paper.

III. "What If"

       follows you around all day
tugging on your sleeves while
reminding you of all the things
you forgot.
She whines and hides her face with calloused hands.

IV. "Not Enough"

      sits in her rocker
by the door at the end of the day
drumming her fingers
and sipping her sea nettle tea,
glaring at you
because you forgot
something
she whispered
on your way out.

Diagnosis

"There's something stuck in your affect and when it lifts, you'll be fine." Dr. G. C

It's that long slide
from hopeful to bereft
as the gaudy landscape of my life falters in hallways.

Doctors offer their gifts: Prozac, Zoloft, Paxil, Buspar—
six weeks of one and six weeks of another until
the gods of serotonin and dopamine push me back into the light.

When my spirit soars with easy smiles and ready laughs,
the doctors shake their heads, mutter
manic, bipolar II.

I lose my vocabulary.
I gain 50 pounds.
I undress alone in the dark.

New drugs tamp me down to some arbitrary normal.
Life spreads itself before me,
daily postcards of people and plans.

I feel nothing
except the smooth surface of the picture,
unable to enter its world.

Bike Ride

When my husband tells me I'm a failure,
I'm riding into the wind.
Push pedals down through air heavy
as wet sand, heave pedals up.
One mile, two miles
I seek relief in the rhythm of exercise.

When I have a good day,
when I think new pills might work,
the wind propels me effortlessly.
I ply grace from the sun.
One mile, two miles
my pace resolute, legs begin to sing.

When a smooth straight-away dead-ends in a pot-holed alley
I feel lost again.
Hope squeaks and scrapes the ground.
I'm riding into the wind on two flat tires.

Kite Without A String

Like peeling away deep bruises on an apple,
I shaved and shaved to salvage some fruit—
a mere sliver remained in my palm.
We were a bland stew, a sprawling hedge, a party you can't wait
to leave.

I wanted a best friend.
He wanted sex on demand.
He said intimacy was being naked in bed.
I said intimacy was a soul connection.

Even lying side-by-side
we could not touch each other.

My Husband Tells Me How He Feels

"Tell me about despair, yours, and I will tell you mine."
-Mary Oliver

Will you be in bed? Will you feel good?
Will you tell me you think the meds
are finally working? Or will you have
that hideous scarf
wrapped around your head
holding that blue ice pack?

The minister said I have a right to tell you how I feel.
How hard it's been on me,
this whole depression thing.
I never know
what I'm coming home to.

Well, I've heard it all before.
Each new pill, and you think
it's going to work.
Now the doctors say
you're bipolar....Why didn't
you ever hear that before?

Years of this mess,
screwing with our lives.
My alcoholism was one thing.
But this depression? This migraine?
Our kids will be scarred forever.

This wasn't in the contract
when we got married.
I never signed up for this.
When is it all going to end?

Just go away.
Maybe that's what you need.
We could all manage without you.
Come back
when you're normal.

The Long Trajectory of Therapy Starts with Questions

*Can you see yourself with your husband when you're
75?*

Like a bell that rings as soon as the door is nudged,
I say

"I can't see myself with him when I'm
55."

Like searching for the pocket door in a remodeled room, you miss
some of the clues.

"Will I be depressed
forever?"

*The patients who never get better live with stress they can't
change.*

Like missing the sign that directs you to push instead of pull, I'm
stuck when I answer

"A constant theme in my marriage is the issue of
control."

When a fire is burning, smoke makes the exit hard to find.

*A lot of women would get better if they would just
leave.*

Afternoon Resolve

Following the stream
of memories I return
to the girl I was
tossing a ball and jacks
on rough brick steps
then ditching my toys
I tip-toe into my mother's
cheerless bedroom, sitting beside her
I rub her back
tracing circles over and over
her groggy words tumbling out
Sorry for always sleeping when you get home.

What saddened me more
than her sleeping
was the empty space
where she should have stood—
in line waiting for the teachers' conferences,
helping out during playground duty,
shopping for Saturday bargains.

And now these dark afternoons
I lie in bed sick with pounding migraine
my own child-self
pushes me out of bed
before my children come home
somehow prodding me help at Girl Scout meetings,
somehow cheering for my son's marching band.

My daughter slides a card under the door
with the sun peeking out from behind dark storm clouds.
Inside she writes—"I know you want to shine."
My son says, "Keep going, Mom. When your legs are tired
and you want to quit,
you're almost home."

The Cobalt Valley

If Depression were a valley
the sun would shine at night
because everyone knows
depressives can't sleep.
Call them light-seekers.

Light-seekers hunker in
the cobalt valley of Depression
locked in caves of stone silence,
gray, cold, and trapped
for lack of keys.

The secret of the valley called Depression—
light seekers already possess
the keys they search for.
They just need to remember
one thing, one perfect memory.

Of hot fudge so sweet your toes curl,
love so pure your heart flowers,
talent so great
even the sunflowers bow
when you walk by.

Advice

The confident doctor in the white coat
tells me to ignore

the suicidal ideation. *Just stop
thinking about those things.*

He clicks his pen,
clips it to my chart

rushes me out of his office.
I forget to ask him, Do I force myself to have sex

with my husband just because
it's the last thing that makes me feel alive?

How do I mute the voice that screams
at me to stab my arm with fabric shears?

Or ignore the thoughts about
slipping the pointed end of the seam ripper

under the white flesh of my forearm
and ripping out the veins?

Like the man I heard
last night on a cable talk-show. He confessed to the camera

"There was blood everywhere
and I still couldn't feel."

My therapist tells me, "You'll just have to settle
for feeling average like the rest of us."

Day Treatment

In the fluorescent-lit hallway of the day treatment center
a catatonic woman stares at nothing.
Next to me, a woman waiting in the pill line
falls asleep on her feet. The nurse nudges her awake.

One behind the other, we file into the occupational therapy room
—some of us paint sun catchers.
The catatonic woman strings plastic straw bits
on to a cord.

The OT directs me to thread a leather lace
into pencil-sized holes
lining the border of a cardboard square.
"The trick is to keep it from twisting," she chirps.

I stifle my urge to run away—
Disobeying might land me
in the quiet room.

When I finish, the OT smiles and pats my shoulder,
"You showed little anxiety."
I smile back, but I want to scream at her—
I've sewn all of my own clothes since I was 13.

The smokers go outside for a cigarette break.
Then we shuffle down the hall into a small pod-like room
where cushioned chairs ring a wooden table.
A moth flutters near the shaft of light peeking under the blinds.

Valerie the therapist directs us to talk about our feelings.
I begin.
I feel frustrated and angry.
I've been here for 3 days and still haven't seen a doctor.

The others rush in as if sensing a secret door—
"I feel hopeless."
"I feel angry because my doctor won't return my calls."
"I feel frustrated with the weight gain, the death of my sex drive."

Valerie redirects us—"Keep with the feelings."
We remind her—chiming one-by-one like insistent bells
"Rage, frustration and anger ARE feelings."
A male patient smiles at me and shakes his head.

"Good luck seeing a doctor, lady.
I've been here five days and
I ain't seen no doctor yet."

I don't care about the quiet room or the catatonic woman.
I'm sobbing, shaking.
Do I have to hurt myself before I get to see a doctor?

Valerie answers without flinching—
"Why don't we end the group here."

The Shock Machine

First they take away your shoes
when you come seeking life.
Like a child you cling to your red quilt
inside a heavy fog of fear.

When you come seeking life
the doctors don't know the self you were.
Inside a heavy fog of fear
you whisper pleas of hope.

The doctors don't know the self you were
as they hook you to the shock machine
You whisper pleas of hope and
pray that irises replace the weeds.

As they hook you to the shock machine
you trust doctors you've never met.
You pray that irises replace the weeds
a gift of faith inside your fear.

You trust doctors you've never met
all your other bets have failed.
You cling to faith inside your fear
and push aside the pain of risk.

All your other bets have failed,
there's nowhere else to go.
You push aside the pain of risk
to save the self you know.

This Is An Outpatient Facility

Before I allow him to run electricity through my brain—ECT, my
last option—
I sit across from Dr. Berman in his bare office.

Hold out your hands, I tell him, then I give him my test—
a photo of my family, a thimble, a journal, and a prayer book.

Dr. Berman shrugs his shoulders and shakes his head.
I say, "You're holding my life in your hands and I need to know if
you care."

He squirms and mumbles, "I care about all of my patients."
Then he says, "I'm taking you off of all your meds—You'll have
better seizures during the procedure."

But the next day, Dr. Sheldon performs the ECT. When I ask
Why the switch?
the nurse in charge says, "This is an outpatient facility."

"You're not going to have
the same doctor all the time."

Dr. Sheldon does the procedure. Dr. Berman is supposed to handle
the meds.
No one tells me to start taking the pills when my treatment is over.

Three days later—
I break out in a sweat, clutch my churning stomach.

Dr. Sheldon looks at my chart and frowns,
"Berman says you might need an anti-psychotic."

I back away from him. I met Dr. Berman only once.
Why does he think I'm psychotic?—I tell Dr. Sheldon about the test.

"Berman prescribes anti-psychotics for everyone he sees.
He thinks it's insane to care about patients."

The Hopkins Doctor Diagnoses Me

The Hopkins psychiatrist asks me a question,
then looks at my chart.

"I remember the first time—and the second—when the depression lifted
I felt like a party girl."

How long did that last?
 "A couple of days…three, maybe."

That's a couple of days too long.
You have all the signs of bipolar II.

"What's bipolar about feeling great for a few days
after a year-long depression finally lifts?"

I list all the symptoms I don't have—
No overspending, no sleeplessness, no promiscuous behavior.

Without looking up at me,
the Hopkins psychiatrist writes the new diagnosis on my chart.

Months later, the depression finally lifts after four years,
But the migraine rages on. My doctor
loads me up with Prednisone for three weeks.

I hear the swishing of blood rushing through my veins
my thoughts fast-track through the looping tunnels of my mind

my heart pounds like I've run up ten flights of steep stairs.
I've never felt so out of control. The doctors decide

it's time for mood regulators. I try to reason with them.
The large red block letters on the Prednisone label shout:

Mania Can Be a Side-Effect of Long-Term Use.
 "Look at the side-effects. I've never been like this in my entire life. Ever.

I'm having a drug reaction,
not a manic episode."

But the Hopkins doctor put the diagnosis in my chart
and now I'm a patient locked in a psych ward.

My Friends Insist That I'm Overmedicated

I slur my words. I forget what I had for breakfast
by lunchtime. I get lost driving to the store.
I begin to slip and trip a lot more.

At least I'm not like my mother.
She drinks *and* takes drugs.
I just take drugs.

Last month, Mom fell and cracked a few ribs. What do you expect
at 82?
Then she tripped and broke her femur.
Now she's in the hospital.
Her doctor says she's doing really well. I don't think
they serve wine there---just drugs.
Does anyone insist that Mom is overmedicated?

I'm not like my mother. I don't drink.
One day I'm driving home on Rte. 70
sun filling my car, the breeze hinting of spring.
My eyelids heavy
I can make it, I promise each time
I jerk myself awake.

Swerve
I hit the guardrail.
Swerve.
I hit the other guardrail.
Swerve.
I run off the road and careen in to a patch of gravel.

I open my eyes
see a man and a woman walking towards me.
They are not smiling.
Oh, God, did I hurt someone?
I'm not like my mother...I don't drink.

"Are you all right? We just want to know if you're OK."
I get out of my car.
The passenger side is dented and scratched.
The front headlight is smashed.
The bumper dangles like a loose button.
I plunge into a conversation
and give them answers they never demand.
I'm so drugged, I confess with oxy-thickened tongue.
I'm not like my mother.
I didn't hurt anyone.
I didn't hurt myself.
It's just a car.

I construct a lie—
Insurance covers the damage.

But nothing covers the
blank façade of my marriage.
After the crash, I can't fly away
from the anger inside.
What now
that I am finally awake?

Even Now

I wish I could explain
to you, my ex-husband,
why I chose the weekend
your parents stayed
with us, the same weekend
of my parents' 60th
wedding anniversary.
the same night I returned
home from my 4th or 5th
migraine hospitalization.

Minutes after sex
seconds after you roll
away from me
droning your sad mantra
It's a shame you'll always…
So sad you'll never……

It's all like a movie now
the way I lay in the dark
and feel tears pool and spill
the way your hopelessness
sucks at my spirit
and pushes me
out of bed to get dressed.

Tip-toe upstairs
kiss the kids good-bye
tip-toe downstairs
grab my purse
get in the car
drive to the hospital
emergency room
tell the social worker
I want to commit suicide.

The Energy Healer

I feel like Alice describing
the Mad Hatter's tea party.
Will my doctor believe me when I say,
 "I lie in my bed
for an hour twice a week
while a woman I've never met does 'distance healing'
from her home on the other side of Baltimore
clears my chakras
and talks to me about images and energy fields."

How do I explain that seven years of migraine pain
gradually faded
like the smile on the Cheshire Cat
once the energy healer
described an image she saw—*When I got to five
I pulled out yards and yards of soft fabric--then
I filled the chakra with swirling orbs of blue light.*

I discover that five is the throat chakra
my authentic voice,
my connection to the divine.
But how do I explain the daily
light meditations or how I
fill my own chakras with colors?

How do I explain the energy
shield of white light that now surrounds my body?
How does putting flower essences
in my water
keep my vibration strong?

How do I explain
I don't need any more drugs?
How do I explain
this is my last visit?
How do I explain—after only four months of energy work—
my headache is gone.

When Rivers Decide

My husband grips my shoulders, his questions land hard.
"Do you still want to be married? Do you still love me?"

I study the red line of his tight lips
the urgent canvas of his face.

I mouth the words *I don't know*.
Even as my heart's warning surges, then pools inside my brain's
familiar dam.

Later I surrender to his demands for make-up sex—
when it's over
queasiness roils and churns in my guts.

I ignore my heart's silent witness
even as the building waves of nausea pound relentlessly

wearing away the crumbling mortar.
The aging dam inside
surrenders to the wisdom of the current.

What Lies Beneath

When I think of my ex, I see
a measure twice, cut once for a perfect fit,
snug dovetails kind of guy.
Plumb and level
shimmed to perfection.

Measure twice, cut once.
With the proper tools
everything in the house lined up—
except his wife.

Now when I think about my ex
I hear the rumble of fear
underneath his anger.

The crimson subfloor of the unknown
screams through the cracked tile.
Rushing water floods the basement.

The Final Demand

The labyrinth of our life together—
the dead-ends, the rumbles of your anger
thundering
like the brooding Minotaur.

When you discovered my planned escape,
you bargained with me.
I agreed to your final demand—
Don't show this to your lawyer or we won't sign.

I trusted you to honor your word—
but ignored the flare of pain
from fresh scars, barely faded.

Before I could escape to a home of my own
I found myself trapped again.
Hope froze when the banker warned,
"Your alimony ends in three months. Your home loan is dead."

Instead of honoring our agreement,
you stood blocking the labyrinth's exit.
As if dangling our papers over flames, you said,
I wondered when you'd catch that mistake.

The Portal

Sometimes Revelation comes as an angry messenger
in the middle of a thunderstorm
a fist hammering on the door.
Rivers of rain wash his face,
the terror of loss flashes in his eyes.
His hands grasp yours,
beg for rescue.

Sometimes Revelation comes like a slovenly houseguest,
sleeping in the middle of your living room.
Eating your energy with petty demands —
fluff my pillows, cook my supper.
Refusing to leave until he evicts you
from your stupor.

Before I know his name, he kicks a box across the room,
pounds on the wall, then rages out of the house.
Stunned by his explosion,
I awaken to his presence.

Sometimes Revelation comes in a whisper
as tender as your first seduction.
This time, you see the thunderstorm lurking beyond his smile,
translate the promises into threats, sense an opening.
You slip into a portal that opens behind him and
claim your new life.

Repurposed

I remember another evening
when summer moonlight
streamed in through double windows.
My husband set an empty glass
too close to the ceramic heart,
accidently knocking it to the floor.

I remember how we knelt side by side
feeling carefully in the pearl light.
We rescued all the pieces but one.
He glued them back together the next day—
even broken, it was beautiful.

Now my breath stops
when I remember
the mended heart
on top of his piles of trash.

I rescued the heart
with the missing piece—
so like my own heart
bled dry
from nights of sleeping alone
with silence sprawling between us.

About the Author

Ann Bracken is a writer, educator, and expressive arts consultant whose poetry, essays, and interviews have appeared in *Little Patuxent Review, Life in Me Like Grass on Fire: Love Poems, Reckless Writing Anthology: Emerging Poets of the 21st Century, Women Write Resistance: Poets Resist Gender Violence, Pif Magazine, Scribble, New Verse News,* and *Praxilla.* Ann Bracken was nominated for a 2014 Pushcart Prize. She serves as a contributing editor for *Little Patuxent Review* and leads workshops at creativity conferences, including The Creative Problem Solving Institute, Florida Creativity, and Mindcamp of Toronto. Her company, The Possibility Project, offers expressive arts and creativity workshops for women of all ages, as well as poetry workshops in schools. Ann Bracken is a lecturer in the Professional Writing Program at the University of Maryland, College Park.

CPSIA information can be obtained
at www.ICGtesting.com
Printed in the USA
FFHW021911240319
51215766-56684FF